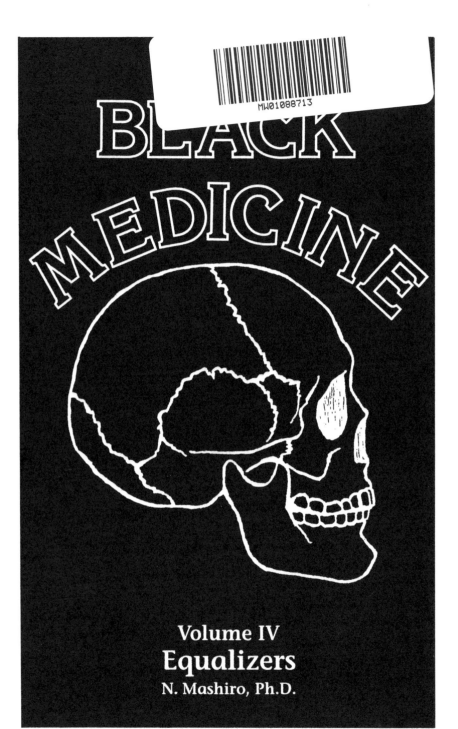

BLACK MEDICINE

Volume IV
Equalizers
N. Mashiro, Ph.D.

PALADIN PRESS • BOULDER, COLORADO

Also by N. Mashiro, Ph.D.:
Black Medicine: The Art of Death
Black Medicine Vol. II: Weapons at Hand
Black Medicine Vol. III: Low Blows

"God made all men, but Sam Colt made them equal."
—Traditional American saying

"The eye of a man is the prince of deadly weapons."
—Owen Winter, *The Virginian*

Black Medicine Vol. IV: Equalizers
by N. Mashiro, Ph.D.

Copyright © 1995 by N. Mashiro, Ph.D.

ISBN 10: 0-87364-815-3
ISBN 13: 978-0-87364-815-8
Printed in the United States of America

Published by Paladin Press, a division of
Paladin Enterprises, Inc.
Gunbarrel Tech Center
7077 Winchester Circle
Boulder, Colorado 80301 USA
+1.303.443.7250

Direct inquiries and/or orders to the above address.

PALADIN, PALADIN PRESS, and the "horse head" design
are trademarks belonging to Paladin Enterprises and
registered in United States Patent and Trademark Office.

Visit our Web site at www.paladin-press.com

Contents

Warning

The self-defense techniques described in this book can be extremely dangerous. These techniques, particularly the use of weapons and firearms, inevitably reflect the author's individual beliefs and experiences that the reader cannot duplicate exactly. Therefore, they are presented *for academic study only*. The author, publisher, and distributors of this book disclaim any liability from any damage or injuries of any type that a reader or user of information contained within this book may encounter from the use of said information.

Introduction

Hello again. I have been away for a long time, but my unfinished business has finally brought me back. Fifteen years ago I set out to write down my personal philosophy and research on self-defense in this series of little books, the *Black Medicine* volumes. For over a decade my conscience has nagged at me to finish this project with the fourth volume of the series: *Equalizers*. At last I have the opportunity to fulfill this ambition.

I proceed on the assumption that you are a responsible person, and that this information will not make its way into undisciplined hands. This volume, much more than the previous ones, contains information that can be quickly and easily put to use, whether for good purposes or bad ones. My comfort comes from the certainty that a person who hurts people for fun (or profit) is too busy prowling the streets to stay at home reading books. Most of my readers are police officers, soldiers, and private citizens who want to learn more about self-defense. It is those of us who will never draw blood except in a moment of desperation who need books and teachers. The criminals just experiment in the field on hapless victims. It is their chief advantage over us, and also their greatest weakness. *They think we don't know how to fight.*

I began the *Black Medicine* series with a simple essay on

the vital points of human anatomy. These are the special spots on the body that are uniquely vulnerable to attack. Everybody knows that a man can be taken out of a fight by kicking him in the groin, for instance. All fathers instruct their daughters about this technique. In *Black Medicine, Volume I: The Dark Art of Death*, I discussed about 150 other parts of the body that are especially vulnerable to particular weapons and attacks. For example, there are nerves in the neck below the angle of the jaw that control blood pressure to the brain. A light blow into this delicate spot can make a person faint, since it has the effect of slowing the heart down for long seconds. I would be willing to bet that very few daughters leave home on a date with *this* anatomic off button in their kit of emergency techniques! Since the publication of *The Dark Art of Death*, at least some of them now do.

In the second volume of the series, *Weapons at Hand*, I enjoyed making a tour of the body's natural weapons. How many natural weapons can you name? Fists? Feet? Knees? Keep going. There are about a hundred more. One of my favorites is the back of the wrist. It makes a bony club to snap into a mugger's face. On the hand alone, the heel, palm, thumb tip, fingertips, first and second rows of knuckles, and outer and inner edges of the palm all have unique applications in self-defense. The soft palm, for instance, has stunning impact on an eardrum.

This was all very interesting, but I soon seduced myself into writing about makeshift weapons, too. Why? Because I didn't want any of my readers to lose a vital fight, and the fact is that picking up *any* weapon gives you a tenfold advantage against an unarmed attacker. Could you take on a professional heavyweight boxer with your bare hands? Probably not. What if you walked into the ring with a baseball bat in your hand? Feel better already? Even a simple weapon gives you an enormous advantage.

Now we must digress briefly. I promise to keep it interesting.

As I have explained in the earlier volumes of the series, I have great admiration for the Okinawan peasants who suffered under the rule of Japanese warlords about five centuries ago. This was a culture and a time when weapons were of edged steel, and the warlords confiscated every kind of blade, leaving only one knife per village for kitchen work. This knife was chained to a post in the center of the village and was guarded by soldiers in armor. Most of this is legend, but it has the ring of truth.

Of course there were atrocities against the peasants. Of course there was resistance. And in the fields at night, men practiced and perfected techniques that would permit them to crush samurai armor with their bare hands and feet. They called it *te, to te,* and later *kara te,* all implying combat using the empty (weaponless) hands. They learned to concentrate enormous force in their blows and to move swiftly to deliver lethal attacks to two, four, or even six attackers in rapid sequence. They devoted their lives to combat excellence, and no doubt many of them died perfecting the art. I have personally suffered broken bones in practice, and my need is not as great as theirs was. (I was not practicing in the dark, either.)

My admiration for these men lies in their creative use of the few tools and implements that the conquerors let them keep. The warlords had to let the farmers, carpenters, cobblers, smiths, and other tradesmen keep their tools or risk bringing the economy to a halt. It should not surprise us that a man's tools became his weapons. This period saw the evolution of the *sai* (pitchfork), *tonfa* (a millstone handle), *kama* (sickle), *eiku* (rowboat paddle), *bo* (staff), and *nunchaku* (threshing flail) as deadly weapons.

The ancient Okinawans deserve our respect and admiration for their courage and resourcefulness. But what about today? When was the last time you got out your rice flail

3

and threshed a few bushels of grain for dinner? Never, I bet. Even so, there are people on the streets of major cities this very minute carrying *nunchakus* and *sais* hung inside their jackets as weapons of personal defense.

They might as well carry stone axes and obsidian knives.

In *Weapons at Hand*, I explained why it is stupid to carry ancient weapons in the street. Would you carry a broadsword on the subway at night? How about a lance, or mace and flail? A tomahawk? A claymore sword? A bola? Maybe you should go all out and get a crossbow! That will keep the bastards in line!

The Okinawans were thinking clearly about their choice of weapons, but many of us today are not. They knew that they could be attacked at any time. They knew that they would probably be outnumbered and unarmed when it happened. They knew that their opponents would be armed, armored, and murderous. Their response was to learn how to reach out to nearby household objects and use them as deadly weapons.

Our course is plain then. On the day that you are attacked by muggers, rapists, bigots, or gang members, *what objects will be within reach of your hand?* Those objects are your weapons. Throw away the rice flail and pick up your fountain pen, your deodorant spray, your telephone handset, your rake, your cane, your flashlight, your tire iron, your curtain rod, your newspaper, your broom . . . and learn to use them as weapons.

I made a long list of such makeshift weapons in *Weapons at Hand*, and I invite you to examine it for ideas. I listed about 200 common household objects that lend themselves to deadly uses in a crisis. As I sit here at my desk I note that the desktop is littered with pens useful as yawara sticks. There is an X-Acto knife only inches from my right hand. At arm's length on the right is a fire extinguisher. On the left, where I have to lean only a little to reach, is a can of spray cleaner. Either would blind an attacker for crucial seconds. There is a small brass sculpture on the desk, almost the same size and weight as brass knuckles. I could pick it up in my fist and hammer on someone's skull with it. There is a telephone handset nearby (the proverbial blunt object), and the phone cord could be quite useful as a garrote or for binding a prisoner.

Of course, because of my hobbies, there are more conventional weapons only a step away. Two swords and a tomahawk hang on the wall behind the desk, along with a Vietnam-era Randall fighting knife. They are really just for display, but they might be useful in a crisis. The shotgun, loaded and ready in the rack on the other side of the office, is not there for display, but I may not be able to reach it when the time comes. In a crisis my weapon is likely to be some innocent object lying quite by chance within reach of my hand.

In *Black Medicine, Volume III: Low Blows*, I described a wide selection of dirty fighting techniques for those ugly situations where you must fight *kara-te*, "empty handed."

In this volume I present the weapons course. I will teach you about the many classes of hand weapons and will present the basic, elementary techniques for bringing them into play. It is not necessary to be a great weapons master in order to give a thug an agonizing surprise. Just a little sophistication goes a very long way in weaponcraft.

In fact, confidence is such a factor that simply picking up *anything* and facing your attacker with it in your hands will in the majority of cases end the fight immediately. The bad guys don't like getting hurt. They don't like it one bit.

There are always weapons at hand. The trick is to know just a few simple techniques that transform these innocent household objects into deadly weapons. It is the *knowledge* that makes all the difference.

Let's get busy. It is good to be back.

N. Mashiro, June 1994

The foot is powerful and relatively armored. Roll back on the ground and *kick*.

When There Is No Weapon

This is a book about how to use the families of expedient weapons. An organized approach demands that we begin with the fundamentals, that is, what to do when you are caught off-guard and knocked down, or when you have to fight in the locker-room showers when you are stark naked and there isn't anything at all to use as a weapon.

If all you have is your own body, what parts of it make the best expedient (emergency) weapons?

Use Your Feet

Here is a piece of advice you will not see just anywhere. For the untrained person, one of the most effective fist-fighting techniques is to sit down on the ground, roll on your back, and stomp-kick the opponent's shins and knees when he comes close.

In *Black Medicine, Volume III: Low Blows*, I discussed this technique in some detail, even to the extent of showing some very effective throws that can be applied using your feet against the attacker's lower legs. The essence of this unique style of fighting, however, does not require even that level of sophistication. Simply drop on your back. Use your hands to pivot your body so that your feet are always point-ed toward the attacker. Kick anything that comes within reach. Don't get up unless it is clear that you have hurt him.

Here's what will happen. The guy throws a punch at you and, hit or miss, you fall down. He laughs and sneers at you. Can't you take a punch? You scuttle in toward him, scooting your butt along the ground and using your palms and heels for support. About the time he thinks "What the hell?" you lash out with the bottom of your right foot and really bruise his nearest knee or shin. You scuttle back just a foot or two, keeping your feet toward him. Usually at this point you will have one heel on the ground and the other foot raised and "cocked" to kick again. If you want to hasten his undoing, you can say something very rude at this point.

The pain in his leg will make him swear loudly. He will angrily try to penetrate your defense by sidestepping and circling. Just pivot on your back to keep that cocked foot toward him. This is a style of fighting that one never sees on TV or in the movies, let alone on the street, and the average person is just baffled by it. As the attacker, you can't do anything with your hands because the defender is out of reach, and when you lean in and try to grab a foot your hands get kicked. This hurts. After a few seconds the attacker will get really angry (due to both pain and frustration) and will lose his composure. Since he can't reach you with his hands he will try to kick you. Watch for it. *Expect* it. When he decides to kick, he will blunder.

The blunder is easy to anticipate. Maddened, the attacker will step in toward you with his left foot, swinging the right leg back for the kick. This puts all his weight on the left leg, and it also puts the left leg within reach of your striking foot. Stomp as hard as you can against the front or side of the rigid left knee. This will tear the ligaments that hold the knee together, dropping the attacker on the ground and, perhaps permanently, crippling his leg.

Next Steps

When fighting from the ground, the kick to the locked knee produces an anchoring injury, one that does not kill the opponent or render him unconscious but which makes it very hard for him to walk. When he goes down, screaming and clutching his knee, you can get up and walk away. My advice is to use the chance to trade up to a more impressive weapon as you seek to disengage.

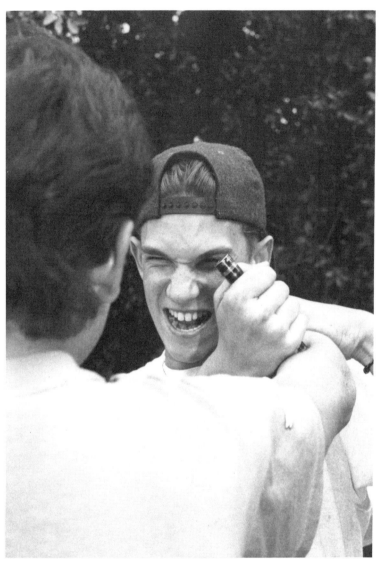

A karate block is much more effective when you use a small flashlight or pen to drive your point home.

Pens and Small Sticks

No one will ever accuse you of carrying a concealed weapon if they pat you down and find a pen in your pocket. Yet you can kill a man with that pen.

In this modern world, which of us does not habitually carry a pen on his or her person? We write checks, sign credit card slips, jot down phone numbers, sign receipts for packages, make lists, and leave hasty messages for our spouses. We would be lost without our writing implements. Usually it is a cheap ballpoint tucked in the checkbook or in the shirt pocket, but if you are well-to-do it may be a sturdy fountain pen with a screw-on top. If you are like me, you may be able to pat your pockets and come up with multiple pens, a highlighter, a six-inch aluminum pocket flashlight, and maybe even a penlike tire-pressure gauge. There are at least ten such objects within reach of my right hand at this moment.

This is fortunate because there are martial arts techniques based on the *yawara* stick, a 5-inch rod about 1/2 to 1 inch in diameter. There is nothing special about "real" *yawara* sticks, so you can just use a fountain pen or any other similar object that happens to be at hand.

How to Hold the Pen
Take the pen and grip it in your strong hand so that about

an inch of the rod protrudes from both the upper and lower sides of the fist. If you happen to have two pens, put one in each hand. Make fists and get ready to fight.

The beauty of the *yawara* stick is that it takes all the force delivered by your fist and concentrates it into a much smaller area. As it happens, the bottom of my fist makes an imprint of about 5 square inches on whatever I strike. When I hold my pocket flashlight so that about an inch of the aluminum barrel sticks out below my fist, the force normally spread out over 5 square inches suddenly becomes concentrated into the end of the flashlight, which is about 1/4 square inch. In effect, this magnifies the power of the blow about 20 times ($5 \div 0.25 = 20$). Driven into the fleshy belly of a muscle (the pectoralis major in the chest, for example), this concentrated force tears and crushes tissue, leaving the muscle stunned and temporarily paralyzed. Directed against a hard target like the temporal bone of the skull, the spikelike *yawara* stick can shatter and penetrate.

And it looks so innocent.

Blocking and Attacking with the Pen

The *yawara* stick (or pen) requires no great sophistication to use. When the attacker reaches out to grasp you or tries to punch or kick you, just hit whatever you can reach. Hammer down on his forearm, hand, shoulder, ribs, thigh, shin, or foot. Drive the blunt "point" of the stick deep into thick muscle or in between ribs, or use it to dent hard bone. Any of these actions will cause serious pain to the attacker.

Suppose the attacker reaches out and grabs your left arm, then starts dragging you toward a waiting car. A martial artist would make short work of an assailant who did this, but we assume that you have not had the training. Instead, use your free hand to grab a pen from your shirt pocket, grasping it in the approved *yawara* style. Raise up the pen like a dagger and drive it down very hard into the top of the assailant's forearm. Aim at the muscular mound just in front of the elbow joint. There is a nerve plexus in this region. If you hit it, you will paralyze the arm for several minutes. If you don't quite hit the nerve plexus, the stick will still crush enough tissue to weaken his grip and let you break away.

Suppose he punches at you instead. Just block the attack by hammering on the inside of his wrist or forearm with the protruding end of the stick. I guarantee if you connect solidly just once, he will not throw another punch at you. That little stick penetrates deeply, and it really hurts.

Attacks to the Body
How many times have we seen a girl in the movies trying to beat off an attacker by pounding ineffectively on his chest with her little clenched fists? He just flexes his pecs and laughs. (That is when we all know he is going to die horribly in the final reel.)

If you take a pen, hold it like a *yawara* stick, and hammer it into somebody's chest, he will not laugh. At the very least, the blow will crush muscle tissue and temporarily paralyze the muscle. Depending on circumstances, a *yawara* blow to the chest can easily crack a rib since the force is all delivered against one rib alone. Every breath becomes agony. Even worse, to my way of thinking, is the possibility that the stick will penetrate half an inch or so between two ribs, crushing an intercostal nerve and tearing a hole though the muscles that bind the ribs together.

It won't kill him, but he isn't going to laugh. Not without pain.

Attacks to the Face and Head
In the martial arts, the normal progression is to break an

opponent down by neutralizing his long-range weapons (hands) and his short-range weapons (elbows) before driving in the ultimate attacks on brain, breath, and blood. Blocking a punch may leave you momentarily inside the opponent's guard, literally between his arms and only inches from his face. Now it is time to do something serious with that little stick.

By now you understand that you can hammer down with the *yawara* stick (pen) and do substantial damage. You can also punch at the opponent's face and let the protruding end of the stick rake across his mouth, nose, and eye. This is not a killing blow, but you can imagine the pain and disorientation it causes. Once you have raked up, you can quickly rake back down again. Or you may "brush his teeth" with it, raking the end of the stick quickly back and forth across his mouth, ripping his lips against his teeth, maybe even breaking some teeth. Got the picture? Try to see it in your mind. It will help you remember the technique in a crisis.

The killing blow with the pen is the hammer blow to the side or top of the cranial vault. By "killing blow" I don't mean that the opponent is actually likely to die from the injury, but a good solid concussion or skull fracture will put him right out of the fight, and in martial arts terms this is a "kill." The implication is that you could have gone ahead and killed him if you had wanted to.

To set up the blow to the side of the skull, rake his face as described above. If you do a good job he will cry out and grab his face with his hands. That's your cue to kick him in the groin while he is distracted by the loose teeth in his mouth. The groin kick will bend him over and pull his hands down low. That is the instant when the stick can be hammered against the cranium with one swift blow. Put your whole body behind it.

Next Steps

Unless you can get in the skull attack, your opponent will not be incapacitated by the pen attacks. He may be neutralized in that the deep bruises or cracked bones may make it impossible for him to fight, but he might still have a surprise or two left. You have to watch him as you disengage, trading up to a more effective weapon if you can, and trying to attract help or reach it on your own.

Leave your pepper gas at home? How about using that fire extinguisher in your car instead?

Spray Weapons

What is a "spray" weapon? If you take your cue from television, a spray weapon would be some kind of fully automatic firearm fired by an ignoramus from the "spray and pray" school of marksmanship. I had the opportunity to try out a fully automatic shotgun once. That one "sprayed" with a vengeance. It took about one second to turn a 2 x 3 foot target into a huge doily.

People who learn about violence from television know nothing.

A spray weapon is simply some kind of pressurized container that shoots out a stream of liquid or powder that you can aim at the attacker's face. Did you immediately think of the little tear gas or pepper gas canisters that people carry in their pocket or purse? That is correct, but the little tear gas bottles are just the beginning, and they are not especially effective. Their major claim to fame is not the incapacitation they cause, but the fact that they cause no actual eye damage. There are plenty of things you can spray in a man's face to disorient and blind him. Unfortunately, quite a few of them cause permanent eye injury. If you are fighting off a rapist in your own bedroom, of course, you may not care how permanent the injury is.

Have you ever accidentally gotten a face full of hair spray or spray deodorant? The effects are similar to tear gas, and the container is good for a couple of minutes of spraying, not just the 10 seconds available in a typical purse tear gas canister. Better yet, have you ever discharged a dry-chemical fire extinguisher? I assume that there is one in your kitchen. It ejects a flowing, billowing cloud of sticky yellow powder. Imagine discharging it in the face of an intruder. Do you think it would blind and disorient him, at least temporarily? You can bet your life it will. I don't say that lightly.

How to Use a Spray Weapon

A certain school of knife fighting insists on extending the open left hand out in front of the body to ward off the opponent while the knife is held in the right hand near the right hip. The idea is to block, punch, grab, and otherwise fence with the opponent with the left hand, then lunge forward with the knife when an opening appears.

The whole idea is to keep the knife out of reach of the opponent so that he cannot grab it and disarm you. The same principle applies to tear-gas pens and other small spray weapons.

Don't hold the canister out in front of you like a fencing foil. If you were to hold it out toward me, I would take it away from you faster than you would believe. Instead, I'd suggest holding it above and behind you. Tear-gas devices usually project a stream (like a child's squirt gun) instead of a spray, and you can easily direct it into the assailant's face without actually looking at the canister. Fend him off with your left hand, or better yet hold him so he can't break away, and paint his face with the tear-gas liquid. It will run into his eyes, never fear.

If your weapon is a can of hair spray, you need to be a little more careful about how you spray it. A spray can projects a billowing cloud of droplets and propellant instead of a stream, and this gives it shorter range as well as an alarming tendency to blow back in your face if the wind is in the wrong quarter.

I'd suggest holding the can above and behind you, as before, to prevent having it taken away. When the opening appears, bring the can forward suddenly, spraying the opponent's face from about 24 inches away. If you connect with the spray he will close his eyes, gasp for air, and turn away. If he blocks the spray instead, his attention will be 100 percent on that can, which is your signal to knee him in the groin while he is looking up. In essence I am suggesting that you use the spray to distract him so you can deliver a low kick.

A fire extinguisher has more robust possibilities. As a rule, the little ones you can hold in one hand only shoot for 4 or 5 seconds before they are exhausted. Two-handed extinguishers will fire for 15 seconds or so and can literally fill a room with an opaque yellow cloud. Both kinds project a thick stream of powder 8 or 10 feet. This gives you some range to play with. Just bear in mind that you need a way out of the room or the billowing cloud will engulf you too.

One interesting possibility offered by a large fire extinguisher is the ability to lay down a smoke screen behind you as you retreat. For instance, if someone breaks into your kitchen and attacks you, it might be possible to grab a small extinguisher and flee down the hallway toward the bedrooms. Discharging the extinguisher in the confined hallway will simply plug it with a yellow cloud. The intruder may bull his way through, but he won't be quite the same man coming out as he was going in. For one thing, he will be completely painted yellow, and the powder does not brush off easily. If he gets a breath of it he will be coughing. If he wears glasses they will be coated yellow and he will have to take them off. Altogether, the experience will slow him down, giving you a few extra seconds to trade up to a better weapon or to bolt out the back door.

Next Steps

The purpose of all spray weapons is to blind and disorient the attacker. Usually your next move should be to disengage, flee to a safer location, and call for help.

There are circumstances, however, where fleeing is out of the question. There might be other people in the house (a sleeping baby, for instance), or there might be more than one attacker. This puts a premium on taking the man completely out of the fight, rendering him unconscious if possible. How would you do that?

If you are using a tear-gas pen, use the pen like a *yawara* stick and hammer his skull with it. If it is a hair spray canister, you can hit him with it, but it might be better to take a second and trade up to a cast-iron frying pan. Use the edge of the pan, not the flat bottom, to dent his skull. If you are using a fire extinguisher, simply hit him over the head with the canister itself. They are hard and heavy, and results are guaranteed.

The key is to be ready to step in and deliver the blow during the first couple of seconds after the spray hits his eyes. The window of opportunity is brief, and it does not stay open forever.

Electric Shock Weapons

So far, no one has invented a working "light saber" that will sizzle an intruder into smoking pieces at one blow. In the meantime, we have to be satisfied with the so-called "stun guns." These are hand-held devices that take the electric current from a 9-volt battery and transform it up to 100,000 volts. Pressed against an attacker's body (even through thick clothing), the electricity is very painful and disorienting, but the current is so low that it is not actually dangerous. Many women carry these devices in their purses.

There is a problem with stun guns that you should be aware of. They have been designed to arc brightly, making a miniature lightning storm between the electrodes when the salesman presses the button. "All that *power* in the palm of your hand," he says. "A mugger takes one look at that and runs for his life!" This line of patter sells a lot of stun guns. All you have to do is scare the guy off, you see. You don't actually have to *fight* him.

This leads to a very poor mind-set in a crisis. Confronted by the mugger, the victim pulls out the stun gun, holds it out like the salesman did, and pushes the button. The little sparks zap across the electrodes. The mugger smiles, slaps the unit out of the victim's hand, and proceeds with the mugging.

How to Use a Stun Weapon

Never hold your weapon out for the enemy to admire. He may decide he likes it.

My advice is to fend off the attacker with your left hand while keeping the stun gun hidden behind your right hip. Don't let him see it. Don't let him hear it. Just keep it a secret until the moment when you grab his jacket with your left hand, step in nose-to-nose with him, and ram the stun gun into his groin. Grind the electrodes into his genitals and hold the button down. Don't let him get away. Ride him down to the ground. Don't just zap once and stop.

If he throws his hips back to avoid the groin attack, just swing the stun gun up and ram it into his throat. Again, hold the button down and ride him until he falls.

Next Steps

If you get in a good, solid shock, there should be no need for a "next step." One-hundred thousand volts is fairly convincing. Just walk away.

If you carry a stun gun, you should be prepared for the possibility that the battery will be dead the night you need it. If you push the button and nothing happens, what do you do?

A stun gun is a lot like a *yawara* stick. You can hammer with it against face, arms, shins, and so forth. *Pound* him with it. Sometimes trading up to a different weapon simply means using the weapon in your hand a different way.

Telephones

Cellular telephones.

There you are, walking down the sidewalk late at night on your way home from a hard day at the office. You notice a couple of hoods following you and getting closer. What do you do?

At the next street light or lighted doorway, you stop and pull out your cellular phone. Dial 911. Put the phone to your ear and look right at the thugs. Start to talk. "Yes, officer. There are two of them . . ."

Watch the goblins run for cover.

If you can call the police for help, *do it*.

To use the five-cell flashlight as a club, first shine it in his eyes and then smash a collarbone with it.

Clubs

What exactly do I mean by a "club"? A club is an object that is about the same length, thickness, and weight as a police nightstick. A 5-cell flashlight qualifies, and so does a rolling pin. You might also think of a fireplace poker or a large crescent wrench. A club is any object that will produce a satisfying impact against an attacker's body when swung with one hand.

A baseball bat, alas, does not qualify. Neither does a golf club. Neither lends itself to a heavy one-handed impact. A hammer or hatchet comes close, but we really need something that will strike and slide off rather than dig in.

How to Hold the Club

This is going to surprise you. The "club" I favor for casual nighttime strolls in the "hood" is a 5-cell aluminum flashlight. You can get them in any hardware store these days. Sometimes they come with a little sticker on the side that says, "NOT to be used as a nightstick." It violates the warranty, I suppose!

Hold the flashlight (club) in your strong hand. The lens of the light protrudes from the little-finger side of the hand, and the length of the barrel sticks up out of the thumb side of the hand. Turn the flashlight so that you can work the switch with one of your fingers. On my flashlight the switch is a rubber push-button I can work with my middle finger. Now casually swing the flashlight up so the barrel rests on your shoulder, lens pointed forward. Click the light on.

These lights are bright, and when you point it in an intruder's face you will destroy his night vision immediately. One good flash in the face, followed by darkness, and he will have a very hard time seeing your attacks in time to parry them.

Attacks Against Hands and Arms

Again we presume a basically defensive situation. You heard a noise at night and went to investigate. You have your 5-cell flashlight in hand. Suddenly you are confronted by an intruder who attacks you. What do you do with the flashlight to fend off the attack?

When the assailant reaches for you or throws a punch, try to crack the flashlight against his hand or wrist. Aim for bony structures rather than meaty ones. It is not that difficult to fracture his wrist with a sharp, solid blow. Rapping the flashlight hard against his hand can easily break or dislocate fingers.

Try to hurt him. If you can stop the attack by doing no more damage than breaking a finger, you have won with moral bonus points. A half-hearted effort, however, will not win, and there are no moral bonus points for losing.

Attacks Against Legs and Feet

Most people have a very limited idea of how to use a club. When they see you holding a club they assume that you will swing at the head. Don't do it. You can take advantage of their expectations, however, by raising the club for an attack and then swinging it down into the side of the thigh or the knee. In a fighting stance the attacker usually has one leg or the other forward, within easy range of your club. A solid blow will bruise and cramp his thigh muscles, giving you a chance to disengage and escape.

If the attacker kicks at you (in imitation of popular karate movies), you can give him a very nasty surprise. Strike his foot, shin, or calf with the club—*hard*. The club can break toes easily, and a fractured ankle or shin is possible. Either will make it easy for you to run away.

Suppose the incoming kick is more like a football kick than a karate kick. Smacking the club downward against the front of the attacker's shinbone bruises the nerves that control the position and motion of the foot. The foot just goes limp. There is a great deal of pain, too. Trust me, I've been there. It was 10 minutes before I could walk again, and then only painfully.

For both foot and hand attacks against you, simply use the club to "punish" whatever hand or foot, arm or leg comes within reach. This very quickly saps his will to continue as well as reduces his ability to fight. Bad guys don't like to get hurt. Nobody does.

Attacks Against the Torso

The club offers four effective attacks to the torso. The problem is that you have to get past the attacker's punches and kicks first. These techniques are best thought of as counterattacks you can shift to after landing a good, solid block.

Here's a simple example borrowed from saber play. The attacker throws a right-hand punch at your face. You block it with the club, hitting the inside of his wrist and knocking his arm off to the side (to your left, his right). This "opens" him up for a moment, exposing the right side of his body to attack. Raise the club up slightly—just above head level will do—and snap it down sharply on his right collar bone. The bone is about the size of a chicken drumstick bone, and a solid blow will break it. You may actually hear it snap. If the bone breaks, the attacker will definitely be out of the fight, since the fracture effectively paralyzes both arms.

Here's a more aggressive move for those situations where you cannot afford to take a purely defensive role. Raise the club up over your head as if you were about to swing down at his skull. Fake him out. Make him fling his arms upward to ward off the blow. Then make a fast semi-circular swing that brings the club in sideways at about waist level. Hit the last few ribs on the opponent's left side. Alternately, strike sharply at the opponent's hip bone. Just aim for the belt where it crosses the side of the body and swing as hard as you can.

One of my favorite techniques is to hold the club down by your leg loosely during the initial confrontation with the opponent. Let it dangle a little. When the action starts, simply snap the club directly forward and up between his legs. This move is every bit as sudden and painful as it sounds, but it has to be delivered very suddenly and with absolutely no warning.

Attacks to the Head and Neck

I said before that the opponent will expect you to swing at his head with the club. I think this is an actual human instinct springing directly from our genes. Modern anthropology has shown that our ancestors had a merry time killing baboons using bone clubs. The piles of fractured baboon skulls in ancient South African caves bear mute testimony to the effectiveness of the club in prehuman hands.

I hesitate to recommend club attacks to the head simply because it is too easy to kill the opponent or to do permanent brain damage. Part of my reluctance is due to police baton, nightstick, or tonfa training, in which swinging at the head is discouraged. Too brutal, you see. Damage to the suspect's head is considered evidence that the officer lost control.

Let's face it, if you can whack him on the head you can choose to break his collarbone instead with less risk of permanent damage. And the damage is not nearly as photogenic, in case the spectators are filming you.

On the other hand, I have alluded to situations where you have no choice but to do something immediate, decisive, and potentially lethal to put an opponent completely out of the fight. If I were attacked by a gang, for instance, I would not hesitate to fracture a skull or two in the first moments of the melee. In that kind of situation you have to reduce the odds quickly and permanently. Snapping that heavy flashlight straight forward into the attacker's forehead will do that, and it will free you to turn your attention to the next guy. There is nothing more merciless than a mob attack on a lone individual. You have to be just as ruthless to survive it.

Next Steps

If you are using a club for self-defense, the "next steps" are pretty obvious. You block the attack, counterattack against the collarbone or the thigh, and stand back. Put the flashlight back on your shoulder and turn it on again. Stay out of reach, but stay close enough so you can step in suddenly with that skull-cracking blow to the forehead if necessary.

Why? Because the sucker may reach in his pocket and pull out a pistol. So step back, watch his hands, and if a hand dives into a jacket pocket, step in and send him to dreamland. Then check the pocket and see what's in it. Under the circumstances, you might be better off swapping him the flashlight for the pistol.

Flails and Chains

A flail is a flexible weapon like a chain or an extremely lightweight stick like a metal curtain rod or automobile radio antenna. You use it to "whip" or "cut" at the opponent's face and hands. The actual damage depends on the weight of the makeshift flail itself. A heavy chain can break bones, afterall. The amount of pain inflicted can be large even when the weapon is very light and insubstantial. Even a piece of clothesline raises painful welts when whipped across the face or hands. Imagine what a fishing rod can do!

The essential characteristic of a flail is that stabbing with it is out of the question. You can't stab at someone with a bicycle chain. Also, you cannot club someone with a flail. Clubbing a person with a length of extension cord isn't going to break any bones. The only way to do damage with a flail is to swing it so it cuts exposed flesh.

Attacking the Face and Hands

It is very hard to incapacitate an opponent with a light flail, so the goal is to intimidate him and/or set him up for an unexpected counterattack instead.

The basic technique for a flail is to swing it in a horizontal figure-eight in front of you. Start up high on your right side. Cut diagonally down and across in front of your body.

Let the flail swing up again on your left, then cut back-handed down and across in front of you again. Let it swing up on the right side and start over again.

Just swing the flail in this figure-eight pattern. Both the left and right downward cuts can be used as attacks. Aim at the face, the side of the neck, the upper shoulder, and the exposed hands. If you get a chance, slash hard at extended fingers. They are easy to break and are very sensitive to pain.

Defending Against Multiple Attackers
One of the really nice things about the light flail is the sound it makes as you swing it through the air. It "hums." People who hear that sound usually back off. Make it *sing* for you. It will sap their determination even before the first blow is struck.

From the basic figure-eight pattern you can easily shift to a round-and-round pattern where you swing the flail horizontally above your head. This makes the striking end of the flail whistle by at eye level in a complete circle around you. Speed up and slow down a little to keep the attackers off balance. Turn to face this one, then that one. Take every opportunity to cut down on an exposed face or hand.

Next Steps
The flail is very intimidating, and this intimidation can be used to your advantage. If you cut suddenly at a man's face, he will react in one of two ways. If he is brave, he will throw up his arms to protect his face and try to catch the flail. If his nerve is not as strong, he will turn his back, flinching away from the flail.

The swinging flail is not the real attack. It is only the distraction. Whip him across the face and when his hands fly up, kick him in the groin or knee. If he flinches away, ducking down and turning his back, kick him in the testicles *from behind*. It will surprise him severely.

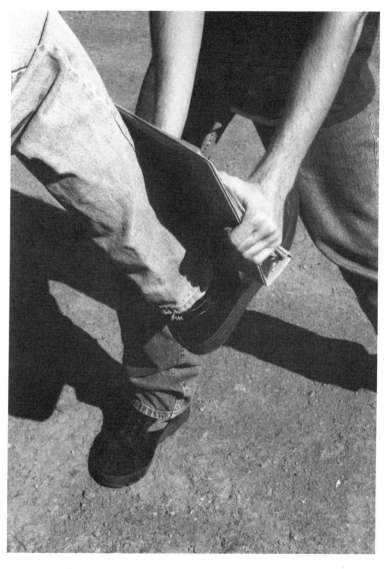

Makeshift shields, such as this notebook, are *remarkably* effective against an angry attacker.

Shields

Shields? Have I lost my mind? Well, not entirely.

Have you ever read the medical examiner's report on someone who has been beaten or knifed to death? One of the first things the pathologist looks for is the presence of "defensive wounds" on the forearms. These are bruises, cuts, scrapes or even broken bones caused by raising the arms to shield the head and torso during an attack.

These people desperately needed the information in this chapter. Their battered bodies bear mute testimony to the fact that throwing up your arms to ward off an attack doesn't really work very well.

What could they have done instead? What could *you* do?

Using a Shield in Self-Defense

A shield is any object you can hold out in front of you to ward off a punch, kick, or stab. There are hard shields, like notebooks and briefcases, and soft shields, like sweaters and pillows. My favorite shield is a straight-backed wooden chair used lion-tamer fashion.

Imagine yourself holding a three-ring binder, a large book, or a wooden cutting board as a shield. Grab it in both hands and hold it out in front of you. As the opponent attacks, just follow your instincts and use the shield to meet the blows and deflect them away. Try to use the edge of the shield rather than the flat side, because this digs into his arms and hurts quite a bit. If he kicks, bring the board down and let the edge chop his shin. You get the idea. These are very natural motions.

The soft shield is more difficult to use than the hard shield. You have to grasp the sweater or towel (or chain or extension cord or belt) and pull it tight between your two fists. Use this band of tight material to deflect or block incoming blows. You can see the use of this technique more clearly if you have a friend take a rubber knife and stab down at your chest. The tight band of material stretched between your two hands really does help you intercept this attack and hold it off.

By the way, only an idiot practices with a real knife. If you don't have a rubber knife, use a wooden spoon. Use a ruler. Use a rolled-up magazine. If you use a real knife in practice, you will be explaining yourself to a doctor and probably a law officer, and you will look like a damned fool. Use some common sense and avoid this situation.

Using the Chair as a Shield

I said that my favorite shield is the straight-backed chair. I love it. Bad guys don't usually practice fencing with chairs, and it takes them quite by surprise. The seat of the chair forms the shield against their attacks, and the four legs become formidable secondary weapons. This technique is especially useful when someone pulls a knife on you.

When I pick up a chair to use as a shield, I put my right hand on the back. Then I grasp the seat of the chair in the front with my left hand and lift it up with the legs pointing directly at the opponent. Turn the chair slightly so that one leg lines up on his face and the diagonally opposite leg lines up on his groin. Now drive the chair forward sharply and see whether you catch him in the testicles or in the teeth. Either will put him off his stride. Keep up the pressure until he is stumbling backward, frantically avoiding your repeated thrusts.

Next Steps

Here is where I have to alert you to a fighting maxim that dates back thousands of years. *You cannot win a battle by fighting defensively.* No matter how good your defense is, the opponent will eventually get lucky and break through if you don't go on the offense and press your advantage.

Shields work really well in fist-fight situations. . . for about six seconds. The attacker seems to try about three attacks before he realizes that he has to find another solution. It only takes another second before he reaches out and grabs the shield. Then he forces the shield down and uses it to pull you into the next blow.

There are two things to say about this. First, when the attacker grabs the shield you must let go of it *immediately*. You are better off without it. Step back and try something else.

Second, you should not let the situation get this far. Use the shield to block the first blow (and maybe the second), and then shove it right in his face. If you get a clear shot you can use your notebook or cutting board to break his nose, but that is not the real purpose of the move. All you really want to do is to cover his eyes for a second so he can't see your legs. Shove the board in his face and, without hesitation, kick his testicles into orbit. It works every time. When he bends over in agony, crack him on the back of the head with the shield. Then turn and run.

The shield buys you time to make a counterattack. Don't waste the time. Use it. Fight for your life.

A broom in the face is unexpected, dusty, and painful. The straws lance into the eyes, mouth, and nose.

Staffs and Spears

Spear. Pike. Halberd. Bayonet. Quarter staff. Bojutsu staff. Pilum. Hastatum. Tales of the Bengal Lancers. Knights jousting on horseback. The romance of metal-tipped hickory slicing through your opponent's vitals!

Nonsense. Go get your kitchen broom and we'll get started.

This chapter is about the "pole" weapons that might be at hand when you need a little help. Brooms, mops, shovels, rakes . . . any light polelike object 5 feet long and about as heavy as a broomstick or shovel handle will do.

The great virtue of the staff as a weapon is that you can attack with either end. This is very bewildering to an opponent who has never experienced a quarterstaff assault.

How to Hold the Staff

For our purposes, hold the staff the way you would hold a rifle with a fixed bayonet. Let's say your weapon is a broom from the kitchen. Step forward a few inches with your left foot. Hold the broom horizontally about waist level. Point the handle toward the attacker's face and let the straw end hang behind you.

Same thing with a shovel or rake. Point the handle at the opponent and keep the awkward tines or blade behind you. For now, anyway.

Blocking with the Staff

Imagine an opponent who attacks you with his fists and feet. You grab your handy broom and get into your fighting stance. He throws a right punch at your head. What do you do?

You have the handle of the broom pointing at his face. If you want to block the punch, just snap the broomstick to your left, meeting the attack and deflecting it to the side. Then, instantly, jab the end of the broomstick into his face, throat, or belly. Drive it in there and then yank it back so he can't grab it.

The same thing works on the other side, of course. Just use the broom handle to rap his wrist or fist off to the side. It is an effective block, and it hurts.

Now the attacker tries to kick you in the groin. Imagine a typical cowboy kick, like kicking a football. To block it, simply hold the broomstick horizontally in front of you and thrust it down so it catches him across the shin as he kicks. Most people won't kick a staff twice.

Basic Bayonet Drill

Staff fighting is an ancient and honorable art known to both eastern and western cultures. It takes years to learn properly, but you don't have the time. For you, basic bayonet drill can be adapted to the broom, shovel, or rake, and you can learn it in seconds.

Pick up that broom and get into your fighting stance. Your left foot is forward. Hold the broom as described before, with the tip of the handle pointing toward the attacker and the bushy brush behind you.

One! Jab the tip of the broomstick into his face or throat. Make it snappy!

Two! Whip the "butt" end of the weapon (the straw brush) around at head level and hit him right in the ear with it. This doesn't sound like much of an attack in terms of a broom, but suppose you were holding a shovel? *Bonk!*

Three! Keep the butt end of the broom pointing at his face as you pull back a foot or two to set up the next attack. Now lunge at him again, driving the butt directly in his face. A typical broom used in this manner drives splinterlike straws into the attacker's mouth, nostrils, and eyes simultaneously. The dust alone is choking and blinding.

Four! Return to your starting position with the tip pointing at his face and the brush behind you. On the way, be sure to "cut" the tip across his face. Rake it across an eye if you can. Raking across the lips is painful, too.

Next Steps

Next? If he still wants to fight, do it again.

The staff is a weapon that lets you stand out of range of his fists and deliver really punishing jabs to his face and body. The end of a broomstick does damage no matter where it digs in. That trick of ramming the broom bristles into the attacker's face is very effective and stands a good chance of blinding him, at least temporarily. If his hands fly up to his eyes, step in immediately, kick the groin, and run.

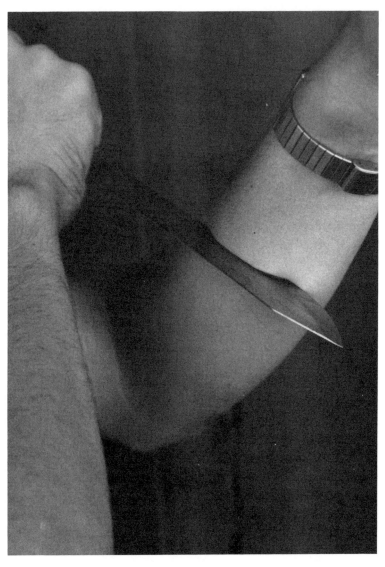

The "light" knife is best hidden, then used suddenly to block an incoming blow.

Light Knives

Here is a tip that might save your life someday. Think about it, memorize it, act it out, and remember it.

You are staying at a friend's house and are home alone one evening. Suddenly you hear a sound and realize that an intruder is inside the house! You peek into the bedroom and see a burglar searching the drawers. He looks up and sees you. What do you do?

Most people in this situation will turn and run. On impulse they simply race away. With just a little more presence of mind they dart into the bathroom and lock the door. Now there are some interesting weapons in a typical bathroom, but it is a mistake to hide there. The door is flimsy, the lock is easily broken, and usually there is no second way out. You have trapped yourself.

Instead of the bathroom, run for the kitchen. The kitchen is the natural armory of the house. In most kitchens you can cast an eye around the counters and walls and immediately see a knife caddie full of big knives. Grab a nice big chef's knife, carving knife, or bread knife. Turn and face the intruder. Now if he comes after you, all you have to do is . . . what?

How do you use a kitchen knife to ward off an attacker? Most people know nothing about knife fighting. Let's start learning.

The Invisible Knife

This chapter is about *light* knives used for self-defense. By "light" knives I mean any knife whose blade is thin enough that it is likely to bend or snap off if you try to stab with it. This would include most kitchen knives, steak knives, small pocket knives, folding razors, filleting knives, and similar blades. They are great for slashing but poor for stabbing.

The light knife can be used to jab at the face and eyes, and if you connect with an eye you can pretty much do whatever you want afterward. Even so, it is mainly useful for slashing, and this means it has the disadvantage of all edge weapons—it is slow, and the opponent can see it coming and block or dodge it. Worse, a skillful opponent can beat you to the punch, stabbing or punching directly at you while you slash in return.

Therefore I advocate a sneaky style of light-knife technique. The principle is that the opponent should not see the knife at all until it is coming *out* of him. This robs him of his advantage and permits the edge to carry the day. This is a good trick. How do you make it happen?

How to Hold the Light Knife

Take the knife in your strong hand. Hold it with the blade pointing down, like an ice pick. Turn the knife so that the sharp edge of the blade faces forward, away from you.

Any trained fighter who sees you hold the knife this way will immediately tell you that you are doing it wrong. Ignore him. The world is full of people who know half the story.

A person who holds a knife point-down is almost certainly an ignoramus who intends to stab downward into the opponent's chest. This move is not particularly sound since it is easy to block the descending hand, and the point of the knife has trouble penetrating the ribs from this upward angle. And the attack is slow, very slow.

44

But we know that the light knife is not really useful for stabbing anyway, so we must have something else in mind. Here it comes.

Drop your knife hand to your side in a relaxed manner. Twist your wrist slightly to place the blade up against the back of your forearm. Cover the pommel with your thumb and fingers. This makes the knife almost invisible from the front, and it isn't any too easy to see from any other angle, either. If the situation is dark or lit by strong lights that cast deep shadows, you can rest assured that the knife will simply disappear from the attacker's point of view.

That's how you set up the magical knife trick. You keep the knife hidden until the opponent is within reach.

Then what do you do?

Attacking the Forearms

The opponent may reach out to grab you or to punch at your face. Block the move with your forearm. This is pretty simple if he is trying to grab you, or you might get hit a couple of times before you manage to block a punch. It all depends on how much karate background you have (and maybe on how drunk the attacker is).

The trick, of course, is to block with your knife hand. You can throw up your arm in a natural defensive gesture to ward off the attack, and this motion puts the knife blade solidly between your forearm and the attacker's forearm. If you have been following directions, the edge of the blade will be facing out and will slice through the skin, muscles, and tendons of the inside of his wrist.

The muscles of the forearm operate the fingers the way a puppeteer operates a marionette. Muscles in the forearm contract, and the fingers dance due to tendons that run down the forearm, through the palm of the hand, and out into the fingers. Just hold out your right hand and press the fingers of your left hand against the inside of your right wrist. Now wiggle your right fingers. You will feel the tendons wiggling around under the skin.

This attack severs these tendons and renders the hand useless. It also causes a lot of pain and a spray of blood, and it comes as a total surprise. Best of all, the attacker will probably use his uninjured hand to put pressure on the injury, effectively putting both hands out of action.

But it has to be a surprise! Keep the knife out of sight until the last possible second. Then slash *hard*, and make it count. Make the edge scrape against the bone. After all, you didn't start this.

Attacking the Face and Neck

There are two other obvious applications for this hidden knife. Assuming that you have the knife in your right hand, you might block his punch as described above and then immediately counterattack by punching him in the face with your right fist.

If you deliberately miss his head so that your fist sails forcefully past his right ear, you will note that the blade of the knife slashes the side of the neck or the face (lips, nose, or eyes). The slice to the neck can be fatal if you cut the carotid artery just under the angle of the jaw. The face attack is very painful, carries with it the fear of scarring, and causes vision problems if you cut an eyebrow or eyelid (blood gets in the eye).

Freeing the Knife Hand

Suppose the attacker grabs your knife hand (your right wrist) before you can get the knife into play. What do you do then?

Experiment with a friend using a rubber knife, ruler, or some other harmless object instead of a real knife. You will find that it is fairly easy to bring the edge of the knife into play against the attacker's forearm. Just twist your right fist up and to the side (either side) of the attacker's arm and grind the knife edge into his skin. He'll let go.

If he uses both hands to immobilize your knife hand, you can easily escape no matter what the difference in size and strength. Most karate students would just kick the guy in a tender spot, since he has obliged by pinning down both of his own hands to hold one of yours. Or you could just take your free hand and stick a finger in his eye. This works well. Best of all, though, is to reach over with your free hand and *take the knife out of your trapped hand.* Then slash his face with it. It amazes me how many people simply do not think of this obvious move.

Next Steps

These slashes are not killing moves. It is true that the attacker might bleed to death from the neck cut or from a slashed wrist, but it won't happen very fast. You should be prepared to seize your initial advantage and follow up decisively either to defeat him or to run away.

For instance, if you slash his forearm, the attacker will experience two or three horrified seconds as his mind adjusts to the knowledge that you have a knife and that he is badly cut. In this "shock window," you have ample time to turn and run. If this is not possible, it is a great moment for a kick to the groin or a stomping attack to the side of his knee.

If he attacks you again, remember to let him feel the edge of the knife every time he sticks out a hand or foot. He will soon stop hitting and start shouting. At that point you know you have won.

A "heavy" knife can sever a frozen chicken in one clean blow. If you use it for self-defense, aim at fingers.

Heavy Knives

Heavy knifes are a special class of weapons that don't come to hand that often. The original, full-size Bowie knife is a "heavy" knife. A kitchen cleaver comes close. A machete is a little long for our purposes, but it has the same sense of chopping power. During World War II the British issued a short machete they called a "smatchet" that is exactly what I have in mind. A large, heavy chef's knife will do in a pinch.

Suppose we offer this criterion for a heavy knife: if the knife can chop a chicken in half with one blow, it's a heavy knife. (For the anal-retentive, I mean a 2-pound supermarket fryer, unwrapped and thawed, on a wooden chopping block, cut crosswise through the back between the wings and the legs.)

How to Use a Heavy Knife
A heavy knife is a club with a sharp edge. You chop with it. The feeling is like chopping at a piece of firewood with a hatchet. The heavy knife can cut or break bone where the light knife can only slice soft tissue.

Defending Against Punches and Kicks
If the attacker tries to kick you, step back away from the kick and chop down hard at his shin bone. Be prepared to

yank the knife back out of the wound. It may sink into the bone and get stuck.

Punches are deflected by chopping at the wrists and forearms. Don't expect to cut off a hand like they do in the movies. According to legend, Jim Bowie could literally "disarm" a man with his knife, but most people should not expect the same results.

Attacks to the Hands, Shoulders, Neck, and Head

You probably can't cut off an arm with this knife, but fingers are another matter. If the opponent sticks out a hand toward you (holding a weapon, for instance), you can chop at it with a good chance of cutting, breaking, or even severing one or more fingers. This tends to be very distracting to the severee.

The chop to the hand (or forearm) usually opens up an opportunity to attack the shoulders, neck, or head. The heavy knife is capable of severing the collarbone, and this is my preferred target. A broken collarbone ends the fight, and for self-defense purposes that is enough.

For more serious situations, the heavy knife can be used against the neck or skull. A solid blow against the side of the neck just below the angle of the jaw can cut deep and sever the carotid artery. (Remember, this is a knife that can divide a chicken with one stroke.) Make no mistake, this is a lethal wound. A man with an open carotid artery drops to the ground within seconds and unless someone gives him immediate first aid, he passes the point of no return (exsanguination) in about a minute.

The heavy knife is a club with an edge. A traditional Bowie is heavy enough that either the blade or the pommel can crack a skull. I would aim at the center of the forehead and try to split the frontal bone. Even if the blade just bounces off, the opponent will be stunned by the blow.

Again, this is a technique reserved for times when it is justified to kill.

Next Steps

Wipe off the blood. It rusts the blade.

Throwing Knives

I put in a chapter about throwing knifes because people are dreadfully misinformed about them. Bear in mind that my remarks are addressed to beginner self-defense students who need practical advice about expedient weapons. For this audience, the undisputed policy is *never, never, never throw away your knife.*

There are people who can take a very heavy knife, throw it powerfully, and stick the point deeply into a wooden target at 16 or 20 feet. It is impressive to watch. I have done it myself from time to time. Maybe you have, too. If you happened to have your knife at hand in a crisis, and if there happened to be an attacker at just the right distance, and if the attacker didn't flinch or dodge the knife, and if the point of the knife was not deflected by heavy clothing or an inconvenient bone, then the knife *might* drive home between two ribs and create one of those chest-sucking wounds so popular with the ancient Romans. Before keeling over, however, the wounded enemy would be very likely to pull it out and make you eat it.

Of course if the knife does not wound him but only bangs him in the mouth and knocks out one of his teeth, your situation is even worse. You've thrown away your weapon, made the opponent angry, and armed him all at the same time. Try to think of something that is more self-evidently stupid.

This situation does not have the makings of a good self-defense technique. Knife throwing is fun (if you take precautions against the knives that bounce back in your face), but it is unwise to try it in a fight.

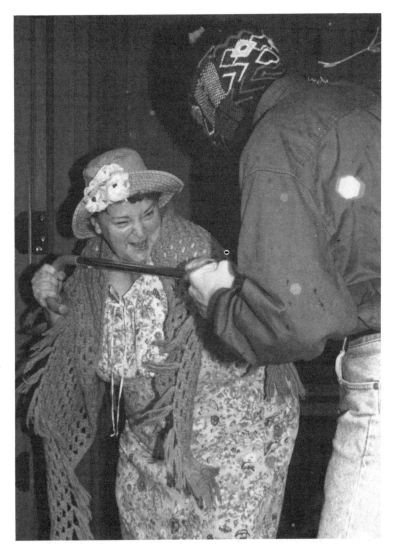

She isn't Errol Flynn, but she knows how to handle her weapon. *Stab*, don't swing.

Swords

Let's clarify a point. If you are afraid that someone will attack you with a sword and you want to know how to fight back, the answer is simple. *Use a shotgun.*

In recent years, most of the swordplay we have seen in the movies has been utterly incompetent. I concede that it was dramatic, but it was not effective. As an example, consider the "light saber" fight in the Star Wars film, *The Empire Strikes Back.* There was some excuse for the callow Luke Skywalker to swing his saber wildly from side to side like that, but the more seasoned Darth Vader should have been able to drive the point of his weapon through Luke's throat about two seconds into the fight. Unfortunately, George Lucas intended to make a third Star Wars movie, so the fight could not end like that.

The point beats the edge. Never forget it. Stabbing into your enemy's face, throat, chest, abdomen, or thighs is much faster and far more damaging than slicing at him with the edge of the sword. This is a classic principle of personal combat with edged weapons. Using the point of the weapon is faster than using the edge.

This principle was drilled into Roman soldiers more than 2,000 years ago. They carried the gladius, one of the most ruthlessly efficient man-killing devices ever invented. The gladius was a short sword hardly more than 2 feet in length. The blade was as much as 2 inches wide, and the edges of the blade were straight. The last 5 inches of the blade tapered into a wicked triangular spike. It had all the grace and beauty of a tent peg or a hoe. It was just a stout, sharp, deadly tool for killing soldiers.

Roman recruits were trained never to swing the sword. The gladius was for stabbing only. Soldiers were taught that a single jab into the chest, penetrating no more than 2 inches, would kill an enemy. Just jab the point in lightly anywhere in the chest. Then deflect the enemy's attacks for half a minute while his lungs fill with blood. Wait for him to collapse. Finish him off with a thrust to the throat, then step over him and jab at the next guy. The Romans were very cold-blooded about combat. They were also very good at it.

For our purposes, though, there is a problem with this philosophy. *It takes too long.* For personal defense we need techniques that work immediately, that put the opponent out of the fight suddenly and definitely. We can't afford to wait for him to drown in his own blood.

For our purposes, a "sword" is any object that is roughly 2 feet long and sharp on the end. "Sharp" may be a relative term. The basic idea is that this object is more effective as a thrusting, stabbing weapon than as a swinging, clubbing, or cutting weapon. For instance, a stout umbrella with a steel ferrule is much more effective used as a stabbing tool than used as a club. The same might be said of a large screwdriver, a skewer, or a long kitchen knife such as a boning knife. An arrow qualifies, of course. Or you might have real swords hanging on your walls as decorations. I have two hanging over my desk. (One is a gladius!)

Once you have armed yourself with a sword for self-defense, what do you do next?

Attacking the Face and Throat

With the sword, you have a weapon that gives you longer reach than you normally have and which must be stabbed solidly into a vital spot in order to incapacitate this felon who is trying to rape or murder you. To obtain immediate results, there are really only two useful targets: the eyes and the throat.

Here you are facing an "urban gorilla" (sic) on a dark sidewalk. He may be alone or he may have a couple of buddies who are circling around trying to get behind you. It rained earlier and you have your umbrella with you. He's closing in.

You swing the umbrella overhead as if to club at his head, yelling defiantly to get his attention. His hands will go up to ward off the ineffective blow. Instead of clubbing him, however, you kick him in the crotch, knee, or thigh. Now his hands snap down to protect his privates and to try to catch your foot. That's okay. Let him catch your foot. That will keep his hands firmly down out of the way as you ram the steel spike on the end of the umbrella deep into his left eye socket. Try to sink all 4 inches of the ferrule into his eye. This is no time to be squeamish.

Will he let go of your foot? You can count on it. Will he fall to the ground unconscious? Very likely. Will he continue the fight? Hardly a person on Earth could continue to fight after receiving this blow, but if he does you can always take aim at the other eye. Will he die? Yes, he just might. This is not a technique you use on friends who are just fooling around.

The alternate target is the throat. You want to hit the Adam's apple or the soft area just below it. If you can ram the umbrella into this area, or better yet impale this area with something sharp, you will give the attacker far more immediate things to think about than the momentary pleasure of plundering your wallet. If you crush the larynx or windpipe with the ferrule, his pain will be intense and he will begin to gag and choke. If you impale him here (as with the point of a big screwdriver), he will be choking on blood. Either way, his hands will go to his throat and his mind will focus on his own survival. Throat injuries are life-threatening.

Attacking the Thighs

The idea is to use the sword for personal defense. One strategy for self-defense is to injure the attacker's leg(s) and then run. It is a good strategy, being both tactically and morally sound. It is usually fairly easy to accomplish, too.

I would not go after an opponent's thighs with a blunt spike like an umbrella ferrule, but a sharp screwdriver, wood chisel, icepick, or long knife might work pretty well. A wound in the belly of a muscle tends to paralyze (weaken) it, and it seems to paralyze the same muscle on the opposite leg for good measure. You can thrust the point of the weapon pretty much anywhere in the top of the attacker's thigh, but the really sensitive spot is on the inside of the thigh up near the genitals. There are important muscles, large nerves and blood vessels there. Cut or bruise that nerve bundle and you can just walk away without a further concern. Your enemy may not walk normally again . . . ever. If you cut the femoral artery, he may die right there on the sidewalk in a matter of minutes. These are not games for kids.

Blocking Attacks with the Sword

The point beats the edge. It is a subtle distinction, but most untrained punches are "edge" attacks. They wind up, swing out in an arc, and strike at the face with a distinctly sideways, slashing motion. Think of any movie fight you ever saw John Wayne in. Those swinging punches are powerful, but they take almost a full second to deliver. What should you be doing during that endless second?

Stab at something. Anything. Dig that umbrella ferrule into his chest muscles. It will hurt him. Jab at his face or throat. Jab the point into his groin or belly. Just poke him good and hard every time he cocks his elbow back and starts to punch. He will quickly decide that he doesn't want to do that anymore. He will try to grab the umbrella (or whatever you are using). That's okay. If he grabs the umbrella, just hold on to it tightly with both hands and kick him in the groin. He'll let go and grab his crotch. That's when you get your shot at his face or throat.

Next Steps

I assume that you have scored a telling blow with your sword or with a kick to the groin. If the bad guy has fallen to the pavement, you should just run away (or turn to fight the next guy).

If he is still on his feet, however, you may need to cripple him so you can run away. You have to make a judgment call. There he is, preoccupied for the moment with his new adventure in pain, but you may have only seconds before he lunges at you again. What should you do?

Step quickly to his side and stomp as hard as you can on the side of his knee. Try to break the knee by making it bend sideways. Even a poorly executed kick will cause enough pain to put him on the ground. That's when you take off running. Your job is to protect yourself, not to "finish him off" with your sword. You can't mount his head on the den wall anyway. Just clear out.

The "hook" of a hatchetlike weapon is used to deflect and control incoming blows. The next move is a backhand that removes teeth.

Hatchets

I suppose it is apparent to you that I find personal combat very interesting. This is no secret. On the subject of hatchets, however, I have to make a confession. Hatchets horrify me. The main purpose of a hatchet as a weapon is to spill a man's brains. I prefer my brains left where they are, thank you.

For our purposes, a hatchet is an axelike object heavy enough to crack or split a skull but small enough to wield with one hand. Also, a hatchet has a head that protrudes to one side (or both sides) of the handle. This gives it added penetration as well as a "hook" you can use to catch the opponent's arm or weapon and yank on it. A claw hammer fills the bill. A one-handed pick or mattock (for weeding the garden) will serve, too. Of course, this category includes classic battleaxes and tomahawks, if you happen to have one lying around. (Yes, there is a tomahawk on the wall above my desk.)

How to Hold the Hatchet

Hold the hatchet just like you normally would. The intuitive grip is exactly appropriate.

Defending Against Kicks and Punches

By this point, it should be apparent how to deal with

kicks and punches. Just use the hatchet to punish any limb the attacker presents to you. It doesn't matter whether you hit him with the edge, back, side, or handle—it will hurt. The main difference is that if you swing a hatchet or hammer at his shin, you stand a decent chance of breaking his leg. If you do, you won't have to run very hard to get away.

Attacks to the Face

Everyone thinks of using the edge of a hatchetlike weapon to chop and cut. That's OK, but why be obvious? Is it to your advantage to do what the attacker expects?

The hatchet is another weapon that gives you that golden opportunity to wave it overhead and, when the attacker throws up his hands, to kick him in the groin. This technique is simple and really works well. Don't underestimate it.

Remember the lesson about "the point beats the edge"? Try this. Instead of swinging the hatchet at him, jab it straight in under his nose. Punch him in the face with the top of the hatchet head. The weight of that steel head makes a serious statement to a person's front teeth. This is an attack people simply do not expect.

Using the "Hook"

Unlike a club, the hatchet has a head on it, and there is an L-shaped angle between the bottom of the head and the handle. This angle, or "hook," has utility.

There are two things a beginner can do with the hook of a hatchetlike weapon. One is to catch a kick and hold it. As the kick comes in, you deflect it by chopping at the ankle with the hatchet. The critical difference is that you let the head of the hatchet pass beneath the ankle. Then you yank on the handle to hook the ankle and pull it toward you. Make the attacker do the splits as you pull him forward, off balance, with his kicking foot held up high. Most people are not equal to this challenge. They go down hard.

The second hook technique is very good for knocking a weapon out of the opponent's hand. Chop down at his forearm, hooking the arm between the head and handle of the hatchet. Without losing momentum, let the hatchet rake down the length of his arm. The hook will track right down the arm to the hand. Do this with vigor and it is almost guaranteed to injure the hand and/or dislodge any weapon he may be holding.

Next Steps

Are you disappointed that I didn't suggest cleaving his skull down to his teeth? You can do that, of course, but our context is self-defense, and it is morally repugnant to kill a man when you don't have to. A hatchet or hammer is such an effective weapon that you really ought to be able to incapacitate an attacker without splitting his braincase. If you do more, your local district attorney is likely to regard it as murder.

Show some restraint here.

Pistols

For the purposes of this book, we must now discuss the pistol as an expedient weapon. I have to assume that you don't know a lot about pistols but may get lucky in the fracas and scoop up your assailant's pistol off the sidewalk. We can't know ahead of time what kind of pistol it is, how it works, what caliber it is, or even whether or not it is loaded.

What do you need to know to scoop up a strange pistol and use it to defend your life?

Revolver or Automatic?

A revolver has an obvious rotating cylinder that holds five to nine (usually six) cartridges. Most of the revolvers you will find in general circulation are double-action weapons. This means that the weapon is carried with the hammer down, and you can fire it simply by pulling the trigger very hard. You can also cock the hammer and fire the weapon by pulling the trigger very lightly. A few revolvers have a safety lever that must be pressed downward with the thumb before firing. It's just a little black lever to the left of the hammer. Snap it down, then shoot.

Automatics have no cylinder, but you'll see a squarish "slide" that runs along the top of the pistol. Cartridges feed up out of a magazine inside the pistol grip. The magazine holds 5 to 14 cartridges, depending on the model of pistol.

The slide snaps back during the recoil of each shot, eject-ing the spent brass, stripping a new round from the maga-zine, and placing it into the chamber for firing. An auto-matic is usually carried with a round in the chamber, the hammer cocked, and the safety lever on. To fire it, you depress the safety lever with your thumb, aim, and pull the trigger lightly.

If you pick up an automatic in the street, the smart thing to do is to grasp the slide firmly with the left hand and rack it all the way back, then let go of it so it snaps forward. This ensures that there is a round in the chamber (assuming a loaded magazine is seated in the pistol), that the hammer is cocked, and that the safety is off.

How to Hold the Pistol

These days anybody who is serious about pistol combat uses the Weaver stance. For the novice, this means use *both* hands to hold the pistol. This will make a tremendous differ-ence in your accuracy. Firing with one hand is for actors in Civil War epics.

How to Aim the Pistol

It is really simple. The sights are on top of the pistol. The one in front is a single blade. The one in back is a crosspiece with a notch cut in it. Look through the notch at the front sight. Line up the pistol to put the front sight on the target. If you hope to actually hit anything, *keep your eye focused on the front sight.* If you focus on the target you may miss it. It is not intuitive but it is true. Front sight!

What to Aim For

It is really easy to miss with a pistol. Even people who are very good shots can lose their cool in a fight and shoot badly. Therefore the universal rule of thumb is to fire at the center of the enemy's chest. This gives you a chance of hitting something no matter how you screw up.

When to Shoot

There have been a lot of people who died holding a pistol because they could not make up their minds to shoot when it was necessary. They apparently got into paralyzing mental debates with themselves, hesitating on the brink of decisive action. While hesitating, they let the other guy get off the first shot. These people are looking at the beautiful spring wildflowers from the wrong side now.

Tell him, "Don't move!" If he moves, shoot. It's that simple.

How Many Shots?

Fire twice in rapid succession. Pistol bullets are not reliable fight stoppers, no matter what you see on TV or in the movies. Put two rounds into the bad guy's chest and pause. If two in the chest did not stop him, most pistol experts advocate a follow-up shot to the head. Just don't empty the pistol wildly in the felon's general direction and disarm yourself. There may be a second bad guy in the shadows, and you may have only five or six shots total. Use two, then pause and evaluate.

What to Expect

I love the scene in *Sudden Impact* (a Clint Eastwood "Dirty Harry" film) where two cops spit out the following macho bullstuff:

"[With this shotgun] they'll have to strain the body to find the fingerprints."

"[With this .44 magnum pistol] there ain't gonna be no fingerprints!"

This is the "pink mist" myth. If your gun is powerful enough, one shot will turn the attacker into bloody froth. Like hell.

The effect of pistol bullets on the human body is studied scientifically as wound ballistics. This is not the place to discuss the relative merits of various calibers and bullet designs, but as a novice you should be aware of a few simple facts:

- A little bullet that hits does more damage than a big bullet that misses. Watch that front sight.

- There are documented instances of people who, when fired at, collapsed unconscious even though they had not been hit.

- There are documented instances of people who, shot seven times in the chest with a .45 automatic, continued to fight until beaten over the head with the gun and knocked out.

- There is no such thing as a pistol bullet that knocks a man down. He may fall down or collapse when shot, but there is not enough energy in a pistol bullet to push a man off his feet. Simple physics.

- A pistol bullet creates a wound channel that is about the same diameter as the bullet. Even the hollowpoint "expanding" bullets, when they actually do expand, don't make a channel much bigger around than your finger. The bullet actually has to hit some vital organ in order to take the enemy out of the fight. You fire twice to increase the odds of hitting something important.

- A pistol shot in the brain or spinal cord will put an enemy out of the fight instantly. A shot that breaks a femur (thighbone) will put a man on the ground instantly. A pistol bullet through the lungs, guts, or even the heart is *not* guaranteed to be a fight stopper. He may accept the wound and still fight on for several seconds or minutes before collapsing.

Fire twice into the chest. Pause and evaluate. If the fight

is not over, aim carefully for the brain and fire single shots until you hit it. That's all you really need to know.

If the Pistol Doesn't Fire

So there you are, clutching the felon's pistol in your hands. He lunges at you and you pull the trigger. Nothing happens. Now what do you do?

If you throw the gun at him I will track you down and kill you myself. A person who is that stupid does not deserve to live. Just because *you* could not get the pistol to fire does not mean that *he* cannot get it to fire! It's *his* gun. Don't give it back to him!

If he reaches for you, strike his hands and forearms with the pistol. If he kicks, crack it down on his shinbone. Jam the end of the barrel, very hard, into the pit of his stomach or into his throat. *Keep your finger off the trigger, and bear in mind that the pistol might discharge unexpectantly at any time.*

Next Steps

I assume that you are a law-abiding citizen in extraordinary circumstances. Bear in mind that if you have to shoot somebody in the street, the police will not be far behind. If the patrol car pulls up and you still have the pistol in your hand, there could be a fatal misunderstanding with the officer. When you see the patrol car arrive, put the pistol on the ground, raise your hands, and do what the nice officer tells you to do.

Then hire a lawyer before questioning. It's just common sense.

Nobody argues with a shotgun. It is easy to see why.

Shotguns

In what situation would you need to use a shotgun as an expedient weapon for self-defense? You don't usually see shotguns lying around like paperweights and kitchen knives.

Well, I could imagine a supermarket holdup gone sour. Two felons are holding the police at bay while keeping you and several other people as hostages in the meat locker at the back of the market. You take up a frozen chicken and coldcock the dumb one with the buck teeth. His 12-gauge shotgun clatters to the floor. You snatch it up. The smart one with the skull tattoos whirls around to see what the noise was. Now what do you do?

What do you need to know to scoop up a strange shotgun and use it to defend your life?

What Kind of Shotgun?

There are a lot of different kinds of shotguns. For our purposes let's limit ourselves to the three most common designs: pump action, semiautomatic, and double-barrel.

Any fool can recognize a double-barrel shotgun, either side-by-side or over-under. There are two big holes in the business end. It means you have, at most, two shots. (Use them wisely, unless you just happen to have extra shells in your pocket or purse.)

Semiautomatic and pump-action shotguns feed shells from a magazine tube lying parallel to and beneath the barrel. Depending on the gun, they fire three to eight times. Bet on three. The semiautomatic chambers a new round following each shot. You just pull the trigger three times to get three big bangs. The pump-action requires you to pump the sliding fore-end all the way back and then all the way forward to chamber a new round.

There is such a thing as a single-shot shotgun, too. It is hard to picture it being used in a holdup, but nobody said robbers were bright. Well, just release the safety button and pull the trigger. Make it count.

Where is the Safety Button?

This is a critical piece of information, isn't it? You just picked up somebody else's shotgun and you need to fire it. You yank on the trigger and nothing happens. Where is the safety button?

Hold the shotgun in the natural way, with the right hand around the neck of the weapon (so your right forefinger can reach the trigger) and the left hand grasping the fore-end (the wooden piece under the barrel).

The safety is most likely a transverse button mounted in the trigger guard. Typically you push it to the left (i.e., push it with the trigger finger) to release it and make the weapon ready to fire. You have to reach around to the left side of the trigger guard and push it back (to the right) to lock the mechanism again.

Some shotguns have the safety on top of the receiver about where your right thumb rests. Push it forward to shoot.

How to Hold the Shotgun

The recoil of a pistol is overrated, in my opinion. Anybody who holds on with both hands and is more than 12 years old can fire most pistols without discomfort. A shotgun, however, really kicks. You have to hold on tight with both hands and press the stock tightly into your shoulder for best results. If you hold it loosely, you may lose it when it fires. If you don't really pack it into your shoulder, it will slam back and hit your shoulder, and that hurts.

It is not going to tear itself out of your hands if you do your part. Just hang on tightly.

How to Aim the Shotgun

Bring the shotgun to your shoulder and look along the top of the barrel. If you see iron sights (notch in back, post in front), use them. Most shotguns just have a brass bead out at the end of the barrel. Look down the length of the barrel and put the brass bead on your target.

It is not essential, but I should warn you about checking the position of your right thumb. It is very easy to lay the thumb on top of the shotgun, and then position your aiming eye about an inch behind it. Can you imagine what will happen when the shotgun slams back in recoil? This is the old thumbnail-in-the-eye trick. Consider yourself warned.

What to Aim For

Aim for the center of the chest. We are picturing using the shotgun at very short range (across a room). At this distance the individual pellets have not yet spread out into a wide pattern. They all arrive at once in a mass about the size of a C-cell battery. You have to aim or you may miss the guy entirely.

When to Shoot

"Don't move!" If he moves, shoot.

How Many Shots?

Assuming that the weapon is fully loaded when you pick

it up, you may have as few as two shots or as many as eight. Under the circumstances, and because a shotgun wound is very convincing, you should fire only once. Shoot, then stop and reevaluate. If necessary, shoot again.

What to Expect

Suppose this shotgun is loaded with 00 ("double-ought") buckshot. When you pull the trigger, it launches twelve .38-caliber lead balls. The effect is like shooting the guy twelve times in the chest with a .38 pistol. Shotgun wounds have a reputation for ending fights. You can see why.

If the bad guy is 50 feet away, you may hit him with only a few of the pellets, possibly only one or two. This is not likely to take him out of the fight immediately, although it might.

If he is standing across the kitchen from you, 6 feet away when you fire, the shot mass will make one big hole through the center of his chest. It is very difficult to imagine a man staying on his feet after receiving this wound.

What if the shotgun is not loaded with buckshot? It might be loaded with #8 birdshot. At ranges of several yards this load is not going to be a man stopper, but remember that the size of the pellets is irrelevant at short ranges. Six feet from the end of the muzzle, the birdshot all hits in one lump and makes that same ragged hole. Count on it.

Oh, one more thing. If you fire a 12-gauge shotgun inside a small room, it is going to be *loud*. Your ears will ring for a long time.

If the Shotgun Doesn't Fire

You might not be able to get the gun to fire at all, or you might quickly use up your supply of shells (there might be only two). Then what do you do?

That's an awfully heavy hunk of walnut and steel there in

your hands. I suggest you review the section on basic bayonet drill. The butt stroke (step number 2) is very effective when applied with the stock of a shotgun.

Jab into the face or abdomen with the end of the barrel. One particularly nice technique is to slam the butt forward into the opponent's groin.

I'd recommend against the untutored approach of grabbing the weapon by the barrel and swinging it like a baseball bat. If you hit the guy you will hurt him, true enough, but I distrust a technique that begins by pointing the muzzle of the weapon at me. What if you crack him over the head and the gun discharges? Ouch.

Next Steps

Hire that lawyer. If you shoot a man through the chest with a shotgun, you will have a lot of explaining to do.

Rifles

I had a little difficulty picturing a situation involving a rifle as an expedient weapon. In what kind of situation would an inexperienced person have to pick up an unfamiliar rifle and use it for self-defense?

The first thought that came to mind was defense of a ranch house or hunting lodge where rifles are normally expected, though you might not normally be the one who uses them. A woman home alone might get into that situation.

Or you might stumble on marijuana growers while hiking in a national forest and get lucky enough to grab one of their rifles. They tend to be very touchy about intruders.

How about this one. Your date gets amorous and won't take no for an answer. In desperation you grab a deer rifle from behind the seat of her pickup truck.

Well, this is the 90s, you know. Get with it.

I should restate my premise that you are engaged in a short-range personal confrontation. The enemy is only a few feet away. You have a rifle in your hands and you need to use it. What do you do?

What Kind of Rifle?
There are many kinds of rifles. There are bolt-action single-shot rifles, bolt-action magazine-fed rifles, lever-action magazine-fed rifles, pump-action magazine-fed rifles, and

semiautomatic magazine-fed rifles. Also, there are centerfire rifles and rimfire rifles. What did you grab from the rifle rack?

Basically, if the rifle is not semiautomatic, there will be some kind of handle or lever present which opens the action and simultaneously cocks the hammer. You have to cycle this lever between shots to eject spent cartridges and to chamber new ones.

Semiautos chamber a new round after each shot. Usually there is a relatively small handle on the bolt, about big enough to get one finger around, that is used to cycle the bolt to load the first cartridge from the magazine. Just yank it all the way back and let go. You've seen them do it a thousand times on TV.

What is the distinction between centerfire and rimfire rifles? I have to assume that you don't know, so here it is. A rimfire rifle is a .22-caliber weapon. It is terribly underpowered for fighting. A centerfire rifle is likely to be a rifle for big-game hunting or for military use, firing large, heavy bullets with a lot of energy behind them. One of these can tear off a man's head or arm as it passes through.

Where is the Safety Button?

All the rifles I have handled have had safety levers, buttons, or other safety devices. Some engage the safety automatically each time you cycle the bolt. It pays to know where it is.

Just like with the shotgun, first look for a transverse button built into the trigger guard. Push it to the left to unlock the safety.

Look for a sliding switch on top of the receiver where your right thumb rests. Push it forward to release it.

If it is an "assault" rifle (one with a pistol grip in addition to a shoulder stock), look for a lever on the left side of the receiver, where the right thumb rests. Push it down.

I have one rifle where the safety is a lever that intrudes into the forward part of the trigger guard. You push it forward, out of the trigger guard loop, to release the mechanism for firing.

Safeties tend to be well-marked, easy to work, and within reach of the right forefinger or thumb when the piece is grasped naturally. Just keep your wits about you and you will find it.

How to Hold the Rifle

As with the shotgun, seat the rifle butt *firmly* against your shoulder before firing it. The big centerfire rifles kick quite sharply. Pressing the stock hard against your shoulder before firing helps avoid bruises.

Remember to keep your thumb away from your eye, too.

How to Aim the Rifle

Just line up the sights on what you want to hit. If the rifle has a telescopic sight, look through it and put the crosshairs on the target.

Compared to a pistol, a rifle is easy to shoot accurately. Even a novice can pick up a rifle and hit a man-sized target 20 or 30 meters away. I dare say that you will be able to strike your target all the way across the bedroom if you apply yourself.

Be advised that most centerfire rifle bullets will pass completely through a human body at short range and will still have enough power left to penetrate walls and injure people at some distance from where the shot was fired. It is hard to keep this in mind when your life is on the line, but it must be a part of your thinking any time you handle a firearm.

What to Aim For

With a heavy, centerfire rifle, aim for the center of the chest. There just isn't any better advice.

If it is a .22 rimfire rifle, aim at the chest first and be ready to switch to the head if that doesn't get results.

When to Shoot

"Don't move!" If he moves, shoot.

How Many Shots?

For a centerfire military or hunting rifle, one shot in the chest is all it takes. Pause and reevaluate. Use a second shot if necessary. Hunting weapons contain one to five cartridges, depending on the model, so use them wisely. Military weapons use 5- to 30-round magazines. Some bolt-action rifles contain one shot and that's all. Make that one shot do the job. Fortunately, a single chest wound from a heavy rifle bullet is devastating.

If your expedient weapon is a .22-caliber rimfire, it probably fires from a 10-round magazine. Treat it like a pistol. Put two shots in the chest and pause. The next shot, if necessary, goes to the head. A .22 may bounce off his skull, so aim for an eye.

If it is a single-shot .22, do I have to tell you where to aim?

What to Expect

A .22 rifle has about the same wounding potential as a .22 pistol, which is to say, not much. Put a bullet in his brain and he will go down unconscious. Put a bullet in his lung or even his heart and he might not notice it for awhile.

The large centerfire rifles are a different matter entirely. They fire big, heavy bullets traveling a two to three times the speed of sound. They produce an effect called "hydrostatic shock" in living tissue. This simply means that the flesh splashes away from the bullet so hard that it makes a temporary wound channel that is inches wide. A high-velocity rifle bullet passing through a man's thigh makes an instantaneous channel wide enough to put your fist through. The flesh is very elastic and snaps back to form a narrow permanent wound channel, but organs and tissues nearby are pulped and ruptured. The impact can break nearby bones even though they were untouched by the actual bullet. If this high-velocity bullet hits a fluid-filled cavity, like the heart or braincase, it simply blows it apart.

From two steps away, one high-velocity rifle shot through the center of the chest really ought to end the contest.

And be advised that the muzzle blast from a full-size hunting rifle or military rifle is awesome. In a small room it could literally be stunning.

If the Rifle Doesn't Fire
You know what to do by now.

Next Steps
Lawyer. Also, you may want to see an ear specialist if you fired that shot inside a closed room.

Tactics

There is a story told of a karate master in Japan who was challenged to fight by a belligerent sailor in a bar. The karate master reluctantly agreed to the contest, but first walked over to a nearby table and picked up a large bread knife. He dropped it on the floor and kicked it across the room to the astonished sailor. "Pick it up," said the martial artist quietly. "You are going to need it."

The sailor looked at the karate master for several seconds and then abruptly turned tail and ran out the door. Psychology prevailed. You might think that this is the moral of the story.

You might also note that a karate master can cross a room and break your neck a lot faster than you can bend over and pick up a knife from the floor. If the sailor had been stupid enough to go for the knife, he never would have reached it. The master *altered the tactical situation* to create a game he could control. That's the idea we want to explore in this chapter.

When your person is under assault, it is hard to keep your cool and use your brain. It pays to have thought about it a lot ahead of time. "Tactics" are tricks and techniques you can apply to manipulate a violent situation in your favor.

Aggression and Confidence
Let me tell you about a purely psychological tactic that

works extremely well. Thugs are greatly unsettled by confident opponents. The mugger threatens you and you don't look scared. In fact, you start to grin and circle closer to him. He decides he has made a mistake. Sometimes this will end the situation with no further action.

If they were brave they'd be holding down jobs like the rest of us.

Use of Lighting

Most street crime occurs after dark. One usually pictures a scene where a few bright lights cast deep shadows. Think of a lonely sidewalk illuminated by an occasional street light. If traffic is heavy on this street, there will be a continuous stream of bright headlights coming down the street. Here come the bad guys. They move to cut you off.

If you have your wits about you, it is a very simple trick to shift position so that the brightest nearby light is behind you. For instance, you can back up against the flow of traffic so they have to look into the passing headlights to see you. This illuminates them but turns you into a black silhouette. The light in their eyes contracts their pupils, making you even harder to see.

Why is this helpful? You can see their faces and hands, but they can't see yours, at least not clearly. They can't see the expedient weapon in your hand. It is much harder for them to see your fist or foot attacks, so they can't dodge or block very well. Untrained fighters (you) tend to telegraph attacks through heroic facial expressions. They won't see those either.

Another variation on this theme is to carry a pocket flashlight. When somebody confronts you late at night in the street, shine it in his eyes deliberately. Shove it right in his face and he'll never see the low-level kick coming.

Shouting

Everybody who studies self-defense recommends shouting loudly for help. They also recommend screaming loudly whenever you get punched or kicked. The whole idea is to attract attention, and criminals just don't like attention.

Karate students shout when they attack. This has morale effects on both the shouter and the shoutee and would be valuable for that reason alone. In addition, however, the karate yell, or *kiai*, contracts the fighter's abdominal muscles at the instant of impact. This makes a very solid connection between your shoulders and your hips, passing a measure of your leg strength into your hand blows.

Shout when you fight. Shout something very loud and, if possible, very obscene.

Using Cars as Barriers

Look around when you are on the street. What do you see that is almost always present by the side of the road or in nearby parking lots?

Cars. Parked cars.

There are five tactical possibilities offered by parked cars. Think them through so you will remember them.

- If you can get a car between yourself and a lone attacker, he will have a hard time getting at you. It is very hard for a big, ungainly guy to play ring-around-the-rosy like this and catch the quick young lady on the other side of the coupe.
- Many cars these days, particularly in upper-class neighborhoods, have sensitive burglar alarms. Rocking the car, or even touching it, can set off the alarm. As you run from the attacker, kick a few cars. Find one that honks, wails a siren, and flashes its lights. Use that one for your ring-around-the-rosy game. The owner will either show up on the sidewalk with a gun or will call the cops.

- Many cars still have those convenient tubular metal radio antennas that are so easy to snap off at the base. Pull it out to maximum length, break it off, and then use it as a flail to cut the attacker's face and hands.
- If there are multiple attackers, get into the narrow lane between two parked cars. This channels the attackers into single file as they come after you. At worst, only two can reach you at a time (one from each direction). This is a lot better situation than simply standing on the sidewalk with six people punching and kicking you.

In the chapter on shields, I warned you that the shield is effective only until the attacker realizes that he can grab it, at which point you must let go of it. Making a stand between two cars works only until the attackers realize that they can climb on top of the cars and jump you from the side. At the first sign of this attack, you must break out or your fortress may become a trap.

Keep in mind, however, that you can get up on top of the cars, too. If you are adroit and are wearing rubber-soled shoes, you can run across a crowded parking lot by leaping from the top or hood of one car to the next, probably setting off many burglar alarms in passing.

- A lot of people don't lock their cars. Find an unlocked car, jump inside, and lock the doors. Then turn on the emergency flashers and the headlights. Lean on the horn. Look in the glove compartment and under the seat for expedient weapons. For that matter, look for a cellular phone! Dial 911.

Fight One, Dodge One

One of the essential principles of tactics is to concentrate your strength against the enemy's weakness. Suppose you are beset by two attackers. Would you be smarter to fight them both at once or one at a time?

When two men try to fist fight you at the same time, it is relatively easy to swing around to the side and get one of the opponents between you and the other opponent. Then you play ring around the rosy again, *keeping the second bad guy always on the far side of the first one.*

Run your best tricks against the man in the middle, and try to hurt him so badly that he folds up and falls on the floor. I'll leave the details to you.

Now dance left and right to keep the second opponent on the far side of his crippled (or unconscious) partner. Most people will not step over the body of a fallen comrade to press the attack, but if they do, they look down to avoid stepping on him as they cross. Expect this downward glance. That's when you launch your attack at his head.

Using "Coward Psychology"

When you contend with a mob or gang of attackers, their group psychology can be used against them in a fight. It is not uncommon for the big scary guy to face you and threaten while some sneaky weasel darts in from the side or the rear to cut you down. Once you are hurt, everybody joins in.

It is a good principle of tactics to expect an attack from behind. Karate students practice endlessly at knocking out an opponent and turning immediately to the rear.

So here you are in the tight space between two parked cars. Thug #1 is closing in from your left. Thug #2 is coming in from your right. You are getting dizzy looking back and forth, wondering which one will attack first.

Here's how to take control of the situation. Take a big step to the left, jumping right in the face of Thug #1 with a big, angry yell. Make this so sudden and loud that he hitches back half a step in surprise.

You can bet that Thug #2 will leap in toward your back. Cowards are irresistibly drawn to backs. After spooking

Thug #1 you *immediately* turn around and attack #2, catching him by surprise in the middle of his step. A high attack followed by a near-simultaneous low attack are best. If you get in his face fast enough, you can be through his defenses and doing damage while he is still in mid-gasp. You have about two seconds before you have to turn away from #2 and leap back at #1 again. Make the most of it.

Somebody is going to jump in at your back. The trick is to draw him in on cue and catch him unprepared.

Coordinated Defense

What if you are not alone when the fight starts? Maybe your best friend is with you, or your brother, or best of all a friend from your self-defense or martial arts class. Martial artists inevitably learn to fight alone. There is much to be said for fighting as a team instead. It doesn't take much practice. The trick is for at least one of you to understand how to do it.

Here you are walking to high school with your brother. Four members of the local gang, the Smelly Frijoles, block the sidewalk. It is not just your lunch money they want this time. The big Frijole doubles up his fist and punches your brother in the mouth.

It doesn't matter how many bad guys there are. The only ones that count are the ones within reach. You and your buddy need to stay close together and *fight the same guy at the same time*. Double-team the opponents one at a time in rapid succession.

Your brother is trading punches with Numero Uno. Instead of grimly taking on the other three Frijoles, you should step up to the side of Numero Uno and stomp the side of his knee. You will probably be able to grab one of his arms at the same time. Uno will be severely handicapped for the one long second it takes your brother to kick him into submission.

You will only have a second, but that is all it takes. One or the other of you will suddenly have your hands full of Mr. Dos. Even if you both have an opponent now, you can dodge and dance, looking for a chance to step in and double-team your buddy's attacker. Break the knee first. Then use the knee or foot to the face, or even the ungracious groin kick from behind.

The key is to put two attackers on the pavement, screaming and moaning. The odds are that the other two will suddenly start shouting "OK! OK! We don't want any trouble!" Back off and get out of there. If I were you I'd find a new route to school. Or a new school.

Running Away . . . At First

Let's say you are alone and are confronted by several bad guys. If you are in pretty good shape, my advice is to turn and run.

Why? Aren't they likely to catch you? Sure they are. Cowards can't resist backs. They will chase after you, but they will not all run at exactly the same speed. They will string out along the sidewalk. Each one will be alone, and not at his best, when you suddenly scoop up an expedient weapon, turn around, and attack the man in the lead.

This is another technique for changing a many-against-one fight into a series of one-against-one fights. Put the first guy down, then turn and run another block. Some of the attackers will stop to "help" the guy on the pavement. Make another stand and take out the new leader. If you can put him down and then take off again, the odds are that the chase will be over.

In any case, you don't just run. You run and look for weapons. You look for tactical advantages. You look for any way to seize control of the situation and turn it around.

How to Win a Footrace

So here you are again, looking for your car in the company parking lot. It is late at night. Shadows are deep. The parking lot seems deserted until Mongo steps out from between two parked cars and waves a big knife in your face.

"Gimme your wallet, motherfucker, or I'll cut your gizzard out." He looks like he means it, too.

Well, it's only a knife. Maybe you can outrun him. Maybe not. He looks in pretty good shape. You hesitate.

How do you win a footrace with somebody who is more athletic than you are? Simple. You break his leg and then run.

Take one long step to the side away from the knife. Usually this means you step forward and to your right. You raise up your left knee and stomp down viciously on Mongo's left knee. It doesn't matter exactly how much damage you do. A kick in the leg hurts, and the pain saps strength and coordination from the leg.

Now run. Don't just stand there and admire your handiwork.

Places to Visit While Being Stalked

One frequently hears stories about the lone woman who is walking down the street at night when she suddenly realizes that shadowy figures are following her. She walks a little faster. So do they. They are gaining on her. She sees an inviting dark alley and tries to run down it and escape.

This is a mistake. You already knew that.

The first thing on your mind should be, "How am I going to get to a phone and call for help?"

While you are working on that one, you should also be thinking, "How can I arm myself?"

At this point all kinds of ideas should present themselves to you. What is normally in your pockets, purse, briefcase, or backpack that could be used as a weapon? You should be an expert at this by now.

In your pockets, *right now!* What do you have? Take a look!

So far, so good. I want to suggest a further possibility for those situations where you think you are being followed. If you have the opportunity, you should stop for a minute and explore the friendly neighborhood arsenal on the corner— the convenience store.

One of the best photos in *Black Medicine, Volume II: Weapons at Hand* shows a flamethrower made by squirting WD40 spray lubricant through the flame of a Bic lighter. The flames shoot out 4 or 5 feet. You can buy aerosol spray cans and lighters at a convenience store.

Liquor stores stay open all night, too. You can buy ice in liquor stores. You can buy ice picks, too. Carry the ice pick out of the store in a brown paper bag. Wrap the bag around the handle and let the point hang down inside the bag. Try to give the impression that you have a bottle of liquor in the bag. Then if you have to fight, ignore the bag and stab right through it. The same trick works with knives and screwdrivers.

Many supermarkets are open all night. There are knives in the housewares aisle. There are flashlights. Sometimes there is a tool section with hammers and screwdrivers. There is spray oven cleaner. There may be cans of spray paint. There is pepper by the pound. There is change for the phone.

To someone who understands expedient weaponry, a supermarket is a weapon-rich environment. So is a hardware store, automobile parts store, or even a corner gas station. Don't hesitate to pay a visit if the situation calls for it.